OXFORD
UNIVERSITY PRESS

Tour de France

Max Nichols

Contents

Crowd cheering at 1951 Tour de France

Introduction

Have you ever ridden in a bike race? Every year there is a big bike race that starts and finishes in France. The race is called the Tour de France.

Riders racing at top speed

The Tour de France is a very long bike race. It can take three weeks to finish the race. The riders cycle very fast.

Team racing

Teams ride in the Tour de France. Each team has nine riders. Eight riders help the best rider in the team win the race.

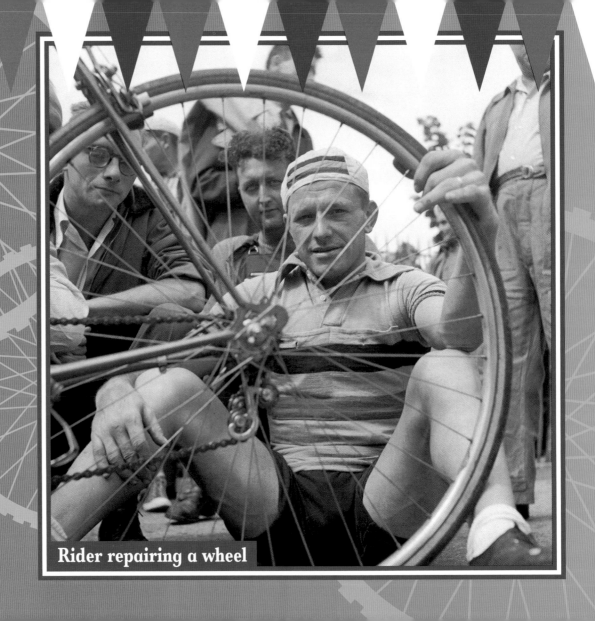

Rider repairing a wheel

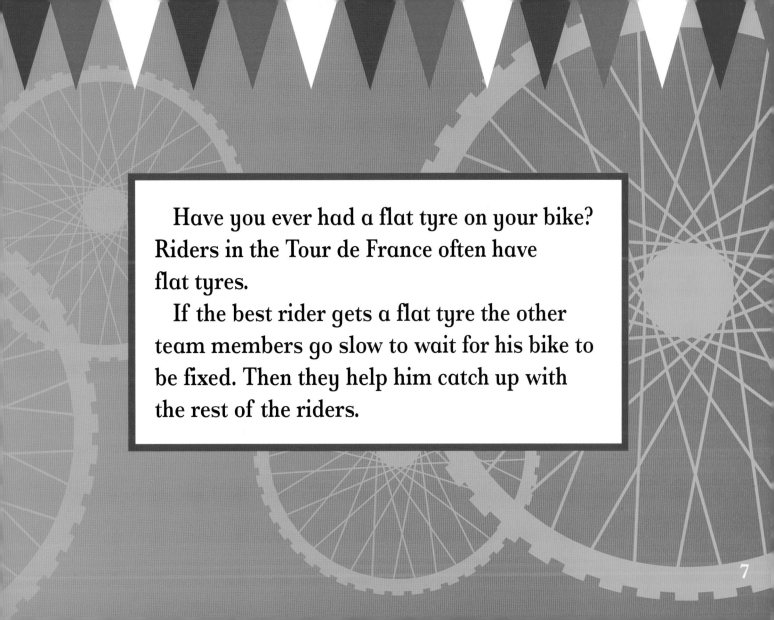

Have you ever had a flat tyre on your bike?
Riders in the Tour de France often have
flat tyres.

If the best rider gets a flat tyre the other
team members go slow to wait for his bike to
be fixed. Then they help him catch up with
the rest of the riders.

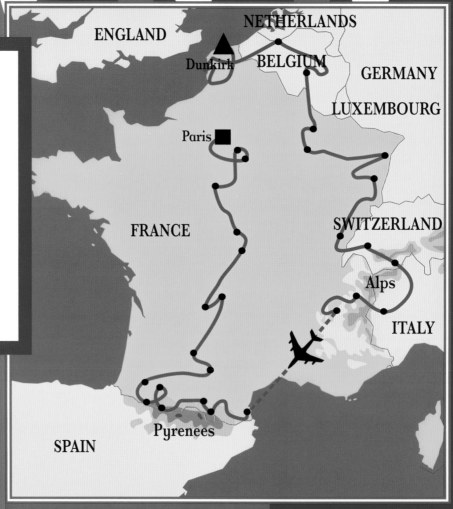

The Course

Key

Course ————

Pyrenees �enees

Alps

Race stages ●

Race Start ▲

Race Finish ■

ENGLAND

NETHERLANDS

Dunkirk

BELGIUM

GERMANY

LUXEMBOURG

Paris

SWITZERLAND

FRANCE

Alps

ITALY

SPAIN

Pyrenees

Race course for Tour de France

The race begins and ends in France. It sometimes goes through other countries as well. The race always goes through some mountains. The mountains are the French Alps, and the Pyrenees.

A race finish on the Avenue des Champs-Elysees, in Paris

Cyclists timed by a stopwatch

The Tour de France race is divided into stages. A new stage is held each day. There are twenty stages in the race. Cyclists are timed for each stage.

Fourteen stages
on the flat

Three stages
on hills

Three stages
on mountains

Narrow racing tyre

About the Bikes

Can you lift your bike up? Bikes in the Tour de France are very light. They have to be light so they are easy to ride fast. They also have very thin tyres.

Tour de France Bike

1. Brake lever

2. Wheel

3. Gears

4. Pedal

5. Tyre

6. Frame

Winning a prize

Prizes

Have you ever won a prize for a race? In the Tour de France there are many prizes. These prizes are coloured jerseys. They are given out each day.

Cyclists wearing coloured race jerseys

The jerseys show when a cyclist did well on one day.

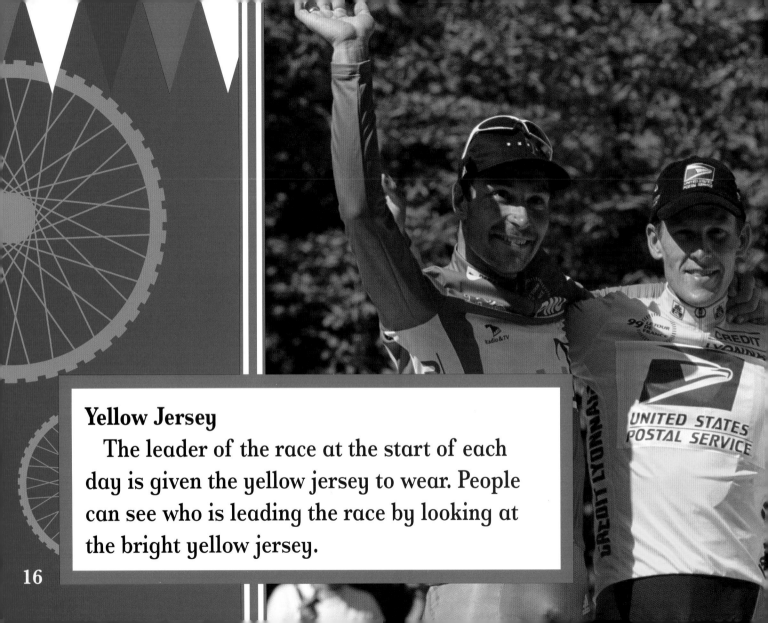

Yellow Jersey

The leader of the race at the start of each day is given the yellow jersey to wear. People can see who is leading the race by looking at the bright yellow jersey.

Red Polka-Dotted Jersey

The red polka-dotted jersey is also called the 'climber's jersey'. This is for being the 'King of the Mountain'. It means that the rider wearing this jersey was the fastest rider up the hills and the mountains.

Green, yellow and red polka-dotted jerseys

Green sprinter's jersey

Green Jersey

On some days the riders have to ride very very fast between two places. This is called a sprint. The winner of each sprint gets points. The rider with the most points each day wears a green jersey.

White Jersey

The white jersey is given to the fastest rider under the age of twenty-five years old. The white jersey is given out each day.

White jersey for best young rider

The fastest person overall is the winner of the Tour de France. The winner gets a special prize. He is given a trophy and he gets to keep the bright yellow jersey.

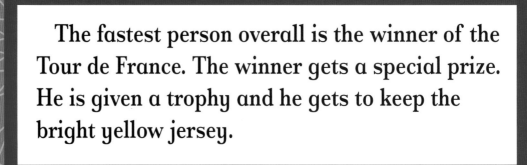

Winning the yellow jersey

Lance Armstrong

A Tour de France Winner

Lance Armstrong has won the Tour de France lots of times. Once Lance Armstrong was very ill. People thought he was going to die. People thought he would never race again.

Lance Armstrong wins the Tour de France

After Lance Armstrong got better he did ride his bike
again. He rode in the Tour de France and he won!

Index